Anonymous

# The Revised Book of Discipline of the Presbyterian Church in the United States of America

Anonymous

**The Revised Book of Discipline of the Presbyterian Church in the United States of America**

ISBN/EAN: 9783337294069

Printed in Europe, USA, Canada, Australia, Japan

Cover: Foto ©Lupo / pixelio.de

More available books at **www.hansebooks.com**

# THE

# REVISED BOOK OF DISCIPLINE

OF

## THE PRESBYTERIAN CHURCH IN THE UNITED STATES OF AMERICA,

WITH THE

Revision of Chapter X. of the Directory for Worship,

AS ADOPTED BY THE PRESBYTERIES, AND REPORTED
TO AND RATIFIED BY THE GENERAL ASSEMBLY.

EDITED, WITH AN INDEX,

BY THE

STATED CLERK,

REV. WILLIAM H. ROBERTS, D. D.

---

PHILADELPHIA.

PRESBYTERIAN BOARD OF PUBLICATION,

No. 1334 CHESTNUT STREET.

1885.

# BOOK II.

## OF DISCIPLINE.

[AS RATIFIED BY THE GENERAL ASSEMBLY, 1884–85.]

---

## CHAPTER I.

### OF DISCIPLINE: ITS NATURE, ENDS AND SUBJECTS.

1. DISCIPLINE is the exercise of that authority, and the application of that system of laws, which the Lord Jesus Christ has appointed in his Church; embracing the care and control, maintained by the Church, over its members, officers and judicatories.

2. The ends of Discipline are the maintenance of the truth, the vindication of the authority and honor of Christ, the removal of offences, the promotion of the purity and edification of the Church, and the spirttual good of offenders. Its exercise, in such a manner as to secure its appropriate ends, requires much prudence and discretion. Judicatories, therefore, should take into consideration all the circumstances which may give a different character to conduct, and render it more or less offensive; and which may require different action, in similar cases, at different times, for the attainment of the same ends.

(460)

3. An offence is anything, in the doctrine, principles or practice of a church member, officer or judicatory, which is contrary to the Word of God; or which, if it be not in its own nature sinful, may tempt others to sin, or mar their spiritual edification.

4. Nothing shall, therefore, be the object of judicial process, which cannot be proved to be contrary to the Holy Scriptures, or to the regulations and practice of the Church founded thereon; nor anything which does not involve those evils which Discipline is intended to prevent.

5. All children born within the pale of the visible Church are members of the Church, are to be baptized, are under the care of the Church, and subject to its government and discipline, and when they have arrived at years of discretion, they are bound to perform all the duties of church members.

# CHAPTER II.

### OF THE PARTIES IN CASES OF PROCESS.

6. Process against an alleged offender shall not be commenced unless some person undertakes to sustain the charge; or unless a judicatory finds it necessary for the ends of discipline to investigate the alleged offence.

7. An offence, gross in itself, may have

been committed in such circumstances, that plainly the offender cannot be prosecuted to conviction. In all such cases, it is better to wait until God, in his righteous providence, shall give further light, than, by unavailing prosecution, to weaken the force of discipline.

8. No prosecution shall be allowed in a case of alleged personal injury, where the injured party is the prosecutor, unless those means of reconciliation have been tried, which are required by our Lord, Matthew xviii. 15 –17 : " If thy brother shall trespass against thee, go and tell him his fault between thee and him alone; if he shall hear thee, thou hast gained thy brother. But if he will not hear thee, then take with thee one or two more, that in the mouth of two or three witnesses every word may be established. And if he shall neglect to hear them, tell it unto the Church."

9. The course prescribed by the preceding section shall not be required when the prosecution is initiated by a judicatory; but in all such cases, and in every case of prosecution by a private person other than the injured party, effort should be made, by private conference with the accused, to avoid, if possible, the necessity of actual process.

10. When the prosecution is initiated by a judicatory, THE PRESBYTERIAN CHURCH IN THE UNITED STATES OF AMERICA shall be the prosecutor, and an original party; in all

other cases, the individual prosecutor shall be an original party.

11. When the prosecution is initiated by a judicatory, it shall appoint one or more of its own members a Committee to conduct the prosecution in all its stages in whatever judicatory, until the final issue be reached: *provided*, that any appellate judicatory before which the case is pending shall, if desired by the prosecuting committee, appoint one or more of its own members to assist in the prosecution, upon the nomination of the prosecuting committee.

12. If one, who considers himself slandered, requests an investigation which a judicatory finds it proper to institute, one or more of its members shall be appointed to investigate the alleged slander, and make report in writing: and a record thereafter made may conclude the matter.

13. Great caution ought to be exercised in receiving accusations from any person who is known to indulge a malignant spirit toward the accused, or who is not of good character, or who is himself under censure or process, or who is personally interested in any respect in the conviction of the accused, or who is known to be litigious, rash or highly imprudent.

14. Any person who appears as a prosecutor, without appointment by the judicatory, shall be warned before the charges are pre-

sented that, if he fail to show probable cause for the charges, he must himself be censured, as a slanderer of the brethren, in proportion to the malignancy or rashness which may appear in the prosecution.

## CHAPTER III.

### OF CHARGES AND SPECIFICATIONS.

15. THE charge shall set forth the alleged offence; and the specifications shall set forth the facts relied upon to sustain the charge. Each specification shall declare, as far as possible, the time, place, and circumstances, and shall be accompanied with the names of the witnesses to be cited for its support.

16. A charge shall not allege more than one offence; several charges against the same person, however, with the specifications under each of them, may be presented to the judicatory at one and the same time, and may, in the discretion of the judicatory, be tried together. But, when several charges are tried at the same time, a vote on each charge must be separately taken.

17. In all cases of alleged personal injury, where the prosecution is by the injured person or persons, the charge must be accompanied by an averment, that the course prescribed by our Lord, Matt. xviii. 15–17, has been faithfully tried.

# CHAPTER IV.

OF PROCESS: GENERAL RULES PERTAINING TO ALL
CASES.

18. ORIGINAL jurisdiction, in relation to
Ministers, pertains to the Presbytery; in relation to others, to the Session. But the higher
judicatories may institute process in cases in
which the lower have been directed so to do,
and have refused or neglected to obey.

19. When a judicatory enters on the consideration of an alleged offence, the charge and
specifications, which shall be in writing, shall
be read; and nothing more shall be done at that
meeting, unless by consent of parties, than to
furnish the accused with a copy of the charge
and specifications, together with the names
of all the witnesses then known to support
each specification; and to cite all concerned
to appear at a subsequent meeting of the judicatory, to be held not less than ten days after
the service of the citations. The citations
shall be signed, in the name of the judicatory,
by the Moderator, or Clerk; who shall, also,
furnish citations for such witnesses as either
party shall name. The accused shall not be
required to disclose the names of his witnesses.

20. Citations shall be served personally,
unless the person to be cited cannot be found,
in which case the citation shall be sent to his

last known place of residence; and, before
proceeding to trial, it must appear that the
citations have been served.

21. If an accused person refuses to obey a
citation, a second citation shall issue, accompanied by a notice that, if he do not appear
at the time appointed, unless providentially
hindered, he will be censured for his contumacy, according to the subsequent provisions
of the Book of Discipline. (*See Sections* 33,
38 *and* 46.) If he does not then appear, the
judicatory may proceed to trial and judgment
in his absence; in which case it shall appoint
some person to represent him as counsel. The
time allowed for his appearance, on any citation subsequent to the first, shall be determined by the judicatory, with proper regard
for all the circumstances. The same rule, as
to the time allowed for appearance, shall apply to all witnesses cited at the request of
either party.

22. At the meeting at which the citations
are returnable, the accused shall appear, or,
if unable to be present, may appear by counsel. He may file objections to the regularity
of the organization, or to the jurisdiction of
the judicatory, or to the sufficiency of the
charges and specifications in form or in legal
effect, or any other substantial objection affect-
ing the order or regularity of the proceeding,
on which objections the parties shall be heard.
The judicatory upon the filing such objections

shall, or on its own motion may, determine
all such preliminary objections, and may dis-
miss the case, or permit, in the furtherance
of justice, amendments to the specifications or
charges not changing the general nature of
the same. If the proceedings be found in
order, and the charges and specifications be
considered sufficient to put the accused on his
defence, he shall plead "guilty," or "not
guilty," to the same, which shall be entered
on the record. If the plea be "guilty," the
judicatory shall proceed to judgment; but if
the plea be "not guilty," or if the accused de-
cline to answer, a plea of "not guilty" shall
be entered of record and the trial proceed.

23. The witnesses shall be examined, and,
if desired, cross-examined, and any other competent evidence introduced, at a meeting of
which the accused shall be properly notified;
after which new witnesses and other evidence,
in rebuttal only, may be introduced by either
party. But evidence, discovered during the
progress of the trial, may be admitted, in be-
half of either party, under such regulations,
as to notice of the names of witnesses and the
nature of the proof, as the judicatory shall
deem reasonable and proper; and then the
parties themselves shall be heard. The judicatory shall then go into private session—the
parties, their counsel and all other persons
not members of the body being excluded;
when, after careful deliberation, the judicatory

shall proceed to vote on each specification and on each charge separately, and judgment shall be entered accordingly.

24. The charge and specifications, the plea and the judgment, shall be entered on the minutes of the judicatory. The minutes shall also exhibit all the acts and orders of the judicatory relating to the case, with the reasons therefor, together with the notice of appeal, and the reasons therefor, if any shall have been filed; all which, together with the evidence in the case duly filed and authenticated by the Clerk of the judicatory, shall constitute the record of the case; and, in case of a removal thereof by appeal, the lower judicatory shall transmit the record to the higher. Nothing which is not contained in the record shall be taken into consideration in the higher judicatory.

25. Exceptions may be taken by either of the original parties in a trial, to any part of the proceedings, except in the judicatory of last resort, and shall be entered on the record.

26. No professional counsel shall be permitted to appear and plead in cases of process in any of our ecclesiastical judicatories. But if any accused person feel unable to represent and plead his own cause to advantage, he may request any minister or elder, belonging to the judicatory before which he appears, to prepare and exhibit his cause as he may judge proper. But the minister or elder so engaged

shall not be allowed, after pleading the cause of the accused, to sit in judgment as a member of the judicatory.

27. Questions as to order or evidence, arising in the course of a trial, shall, after the parties have had an opportunity to be heard, be decided by the Moderator, subject to appeal; and the question on the appeal shall be determined without debate. All such decisions, if desired by either party, shall be entered upon the record of the case.

28. No member of a judicatory, who has not been present during the whole of a trial, shall be allowed to vote on any question arising therein, except by unanimous consent of the judicatory and of the parties; and, when a trial is in progress, except in an appellate judicatory, the roll shall be called after each recess and adjournment, and the names of the absentees shall be noted.

29. The parties shall be allowed copies of the record at their own expense; and, on the final disposition of a case in a higher judicatory, the record of the case, with the judgment, shall be transmitted to the judicatory in which the case originated.

30. In the infliction and removal of church censures, judicatories shall observe the modes prescribed in Chapter X. of the Directory for Worship.

31. In all cases of judicial process, the judicatory may, at any stage of the case, deter-

mine, by a vote of two-thirds, to sit with closed doors.

32. A judicatory may, if the edification of the Church demands it, require an accused person to refrain from approaching the Lord's Table, or from the exercise of office, or both, until final action in the case shall be taken: *provided*, that in all cases a speedy investigation or trial shall be had.

# CHAPTER V.

### SPECIAL RULES PERTAINING TO CASES BEFORE SESSIONS.

33. WHEN an accused person has been twice duly cited, and refuses to appear, by himself or counsel, before a Session, or, appearing, refuses to answer the charge brought against him, he shall be suspended, by act of Session, from the communion of the Church, and shall so remain until he repents of his contumacy, and submits himself to the orders of the judicatory.

34. The censures to be inflicted by the Session are, Admonition, Rebuke, Suspension or Deposition from office, Suspension from the communion of the Church, and, in the case of offenders who will not be reclaimed by milder measures, Excommunication.

35. The sentence shall be published, if at

all, only in the Church or Churches which have been offended.

## CHAPTER VI.

### GENERAL RULES PERTAINING TO THE TRIAL OF A MINISTER, ELDER, OR DEACON.

36. As the honor and success of the gospel depend, in a great measure, on the character of its Ministers, each Presbytery ought, with the greatest care and impartiality, to watch over their personal and professional conduct. But as, on the one hand, no Minister ought, on account of his office, to be screened from the hand of justice, or his offences to be slightly censured, so neither ought charges to be received against him on slight grounds.

37. If a Minister be accused of an offence, at such a distance from his usual place of residence as that it is not likely to become otherwise known to his Presbytery, it shall be the duty of the Presbytery within whose bounds the offence is alleged to have been committed, if it shall be satisfied that there is probable ground for the accusation, to notify his Presbytery thereof, and of the nature of the offence; and his Presbytery, on receiving such notice, shall, if it appears that the honor of religion requires it, proceed to the trial of the case.

38. If a Minister accused of an offence re-

fuses to appear by himself or counsel, after
being twice duly cited, he shall, for his contumacy, be suspended from his office; and if,
after another citation, he refuses to appear by
himself or counsel, he shall be suspended from
the communion of the Church.

39. If a judicatory so decides, a member
shall not be allowed, while charges are pending against him, to deliberate or vote on any
question.

40. If the accused be found guilty, he shall
be admonished, rebuked, suspended or deposed from office (with or without suspension
from church privileges, in either case), or excommunicated. A Minister, suspended from
office, may, at the expiration of one year, unless he gives satisfactory evidence of repentance, be deposed without further trial.

41. Heresy and schism may be of such a
nature as to call for deposition; but errors
ought to be carefully considered, whether they
strike at the vitals of religion and are indus-
triously spread, or whether they arise from
the weakness of the human understanding,
and are not likely to do much injury.

42. If the Presbytery finds, on trial, that
the matter complained of amounts to no more
than such acts of infirmity as may be amend-
ed and the people satisfied, so that little or
nothing remains to hinder the usefulness of
the offender, it shall take all prudent measures
to remove the evil.

43. A Minister deposed for immoral conduct shall not be restored, even on the deepest sorrow for his sin, until after some considerable time of eminent and exemplary, humble and edifying conduct; and he ought in no case to be restored, until it shall clearly appear to the judicatory, within whose bounds he resides, that the restoration can be effected without injury to the cause of religion; and then only by the judicatory inflicting the censure, or with its advice and consent.

44. If a Minister is deposed without excommunication, his pulpit, if he is a Pastor, shall be declared vacant; and the Presbytery shall give him a letter to any church with which he may desire to connect himself where his lot may be cast, in which shall be stated his exact relation to the Church. If a Pastor is suspended from office only, the Presbytery may, if no appeal from the sentence of suspension is pending, declare his pulpit vacant.

45. A Presbytery may, if the edification of the Church demand it, require an accused Minister to refrain from the exercise of his office until final action in the case shall be taken: *provided*, that in all cases a speedy investigation or trial shall be had.

46. In process by a Session against a ruling elder or a deacon, the provisions of this chapter, so far as applicable, shall be observed.

40 *

# CHAPTER VII.

OF CASES WITHOUT PROCESS.

47. If a person commits an offence in the
presence of a judicatory, or comes forward as
his own accuser and makes known his offence,
the judicatory may proceed to judgment without process, giving the offender an opportunity to be heard; and in the case first named
he may demand a delay of at least two days
before judgment. The record must show the
nature of the offence, as well as the judgment
and the reasons therefor, and appeal may be
taken from the judgment as in other cases.

48. If a communicant, not chargeable with
immoral conduct, inform the Session that he
is fully persuaded that he has no right to come
to the Lord's Table, the Session shall confer
with him on the subject, and may, should he
continue of the same mind, and his attendance
on the other means of grace be regular, ex-
cuse him from attendance on the Lord's Supper; and, after fully satisfying themselves
that his judgment is not the result of mis-
taken views, shall erase his name from the
roll of communicants, and make record of
their action in the case.

49. If a communicant, not chargeable with
immoral conduct, removes out of the bounds
of his Church, without asking for or receiving a regular certificate of dismission to another Church, and his residence is known, the

Session may, within two years, advise him to apply for such certificate; and, if he fails so to do, without giving sufficient reason, his name may be placed on the roll of suspended members, until he shall satisfy the Session of the propriety of his restoration. But, if the Session has no knowledge of him for the space of three years, it may erase his name from the roll of communicants, making record of its action and the reasons therefor. In either case, the member shall continue subject to the jurisdiction of the Session. A separate roll of all such names shall be kept, stating the relations of each to the Church.

50. If any communicant, not chargeable with immoral conduct, neglects the ordinances of the Church for one year, and in circumstances such as the Session shall regard to be a serious injury to the cause of religion, he may, after affectionate visitation by the Session, and admonition if need be, be suspended from the communion of the Church until he gives satisfactory evidence of the sincerity of his repentance, but he shall not be excommunicated without due process of discipline.

51. If a Minister, otherwise in good standing, shall make application to be released from the office of the ministry, he may, at the discretion of the Presbytery, be put on probation, for one year at least, in such a manner as the Presbytery may direct, in order to ascertain his motives and reasons for such a re-

linquishment. And if, at the end of this period, the Presbytery be satisfied that he cannot be useful and happy in the exercise of his ministry, they may allow him to demit the office, and return to the condition of a private member in the Church, ordering his name to be stricken from the roll of the Presbytery, and giving him a letter to any Church with which he may desire to connect himself.

52. If a communicant renounces the communion of this Church by joining another denomination, without a regular dismission, although such conduct is disorderly, the Session shall take no other action in the case than to record the fact, and order his name to be erased from the roll. If charges are pending against him, these charges may be prosecuted.

53. If a Minister, not otherwise chargeable with an offence, renounces the jurisdiction of this Church, by abandoning the ministry, or becoming independent, or joining another denomination not deemed heretical, without a regular dismission, the Presbytery shall take no other action than to record the fact and to erase his name from the roll. If charges are pending against him, he may be tried thereon. If it appears that he has joined another denomination deemed heretical, he may be suspended, deposed, or excommunicated.

# CHAPTER VIII.

## OF EVIDENCE.

54. JUDICATORIES ought to be very careful and impartial in receiving testimony. Not every person is competent, and not every competent person is credible, as a witness.

55. All persons, whether parties or otherwise, are competent witnesses, except such as do not believe in the existence of God, or a future state of rewards and punishments, or have not sufficient intelligence to understand the obligation of an oath. Any witness may be challenged for incompetency, and the judicatory shall decide the question.

56. The credibility of a witness, or the degree of credit due to his testimony, may be affected by relationship to any of the parties; by interest in the result of the trial; by want of proper age; by weakness of understanding; by infamy or malignity of character; by being under church censure; by general rashness or indiscretion; or by any other circumstances that appear to affect his veracity, knowledge or interest in the case.

57. A husband or wife shall be a competent witness for or against the other, but shall not be compelled to testify.

58. Evidence may be oral, written or printed, direct or circumstantial. A charge may be proven by the testimony of one witness, only when supported by other evidence; but,

when there are several specifications under the same general charge, the proof of two or more of the specifications, by different credible witnesses, shall be sufficient to establish the charge.

59. No witness, afterwards to be examined, except a member of the judicatory, shall be present during the examination of another witness if either party object.

60. Witnesses shall be examined first by the party producing them; then cross-examined by the opposite party; after which any member of the judicatory or either party may put additional interrogatories. Irrelevant or frivolous questions shall not be admitted, nor leading questions by the parties producing the witness, except under permission of the judicatory as necessary to elicit the truth.

61. The oath or affirmation shall be administered by the Moderator in the following, or like, terms: "You solemnly promise, in the presence of the omniscient and heart-searching God, that you will declare the truth, the whole truth, and nothing but the truth, according to the best of your knowledge, in the matter in which you are called to testify, as you shall answer to the Great Judge of quick and dead."

62. Every question put to a witness shall, if required, be reduced to writing. And, if either party desire it, or if the judicatory shall

so decide, both question and answer shall be recorded. The testimony, thus recorded, shall be read to the witnesses, in the presence of the judicatory, for their approbation and subscription.

63. The records of a judicatory, or any part of them, whether original or transcribed, if regularly authenticated by the Clerk, or in case of his death, absence, disability or failure from any cause, by the Moderator, shall be deemed good and sufficient evidence in every other judicatory.

64. In like manner, testimony taken by one judicatory, and regularly certified, shall be received by every other judicatory, as no less valid than if it had been taken by themselves.

65. Any judicatory, before which a case may be pending, shall have power, whenever the necessity of parties or witnesses shall require it, to appoint, on the application of either party, a Commission of Ministers, or Elders, or both, to examine witnesses; which Commission, if the case requires it, may be of persons within the jurisdiction of another body. The Commissioners so appointed shall take such testimony as may be offered by either party. The testimony shall be taken in accordance with the rules governing the judicatory, either orally or on written interrogatories and cross-interrogatories, duly settled by the judicatory, due notice having been

given of the time when, and place where, the witnesses are to be examined. All questions, as to the relevancy or competency of the testimony so taken, shall be determined by the judicatory. The testimony, properly authenticated by the signatures of the Commissioners, shall be transmitted, in due time, to the Clerk of the judicatory before which the case is pending.

66. A member of the judicatory may be called upon to testify in a case which comes before it. He shall be qualified as other witnesses are, and, after having given his testimony, may immediately resume his seat as a member of the judicatory.

67. A member of the Church, summoned as a witness, and refusing to appear, or, having appeared, refusing to testify, shall be censured according to the circumstances of the case for his contumacy.

68. If, after a trial before any judicatory, new evidence is discovered, supposed to be important to the exculpation of the accused, he may ask, if the case has not been appealed, and the judicatory shall grant, if justice seems to require it, a new trial.

69. If, in the prosecution of an appeal, new evidence is offered, which, in the judgment of the appellate judicatory, has an important bearing on the case, it shall either refer the whole case to the inferior judicatory for a new trial; or, with the consent of the

parties, take the testimony, and hear and determine the case.

## CHAPTER IX.

### OF THE WAYS IN WHICH A CAUSE MAY BE CARRIED FROM A LOWER TO A HIGHER JUDICATORY.

70. ALL proceedings of the Session, the Presbytery, and the Synod (except as limited by Chapter XI., Section 4, of the Form of Government), are subject to review by, and may be taken to, a superior judicatory, by General Review and Control, Reference, Complaint or Appeal.

#### I. OF GENERAL REVIEW AND CONTROL.

71. All proceedings of the Church shall be reported to, and reviewed by, the Session, and by its order incorporated with its Records. Every judicatory above a Session shall review, at least once a year, the records of the proceedings of the judicatory next below; and, if the lower judicatory shall omit to send up its records for this purpose, the higher may require them to be produced, either immediately, or at a specified time, as circumstances may determine.

72. In such review, the judicatory shall examine, first, whether the proceedings have been correctly recorded; second, whether they

41

have been constitutional and regular; and third, whether they have been wise, equitable and for the edification of the Church.

73. Members of a judicatory, the records of which are under review, shall not be allowed to vote thereon.

74. In most cases the superior judicatory may discharge its duty, by simply placing on its own records, and on those under review, the censure which it may pass. But irregular proceedings may be found so disreputable and injurious, that the inferior judicatory must be required to review and correct, or reverse them, and report, within a specified time, its obedience to the order: *provided*, however, that no judicial decision shall be reversed, unless regularly taken up by appeal or complaint.

75. If a judicatory is, at any time, well advised of any unconstitutional proceedings of a lower judicatory, the latter shall be cited to appear, at a specified time and place, to produce the records, and to show what it has done in the matter in question; after which, if the charge is sustained, the whole matter shall be concluded by the judicatory itself, or be remitted to the lower judicatory, with direction as to its disposition.

76. Judicatories may sometimes neglect to perform their duty, by which neglect heretical opinions or corrupt practices may be allowed to gain ground, or offenders of a gross

character may be suffered to escape; or some
part of their proceedings may have been
omitted from the record, or not properly recorded. If, therefore, at any time, the superior judicatory is well advised of such neglects,
omissions, or irregularities on the part of the
inferior judicatory, it may require its records
to be produced, and shall either proceed to
examine and decide the whole matter, as com-
pletely as if proper record had been made; or
it shall cite the lower judicatory, and proceed
as in the next preceding section.

## II. OF REFERENCES.

77. A Reference is a representation in
writing, made by an inferior to a superior
judicatory, of a judicial case not yet decided.
Generally, however, it is more conducive to
the public good that each judicatory should
fulfil its duty by exercising its own judgment.

78. Cases which are new, important, diffi-
cult, or of peculiar delicacy, the decision of
which may establish principles or precedents
of extensive influence, on which the inferior
judicatory is greatly divided, or on which for
any reason it is desirable that a superior judicatory should first decide, are proper subjects
of Reference.

79. References are, either for mere advice,
preparatory to a decision by the inferior judicatory, or for ultimate trial and decision by

the superior; and are to be carried to the next higher judicatory. If for advice, the Reference only suspends the decision of the inferior judicatory; if for trial, it submits the whole case to the final judgment of the superior.

80. In cases of Reference, members of the inferior judicatory may sit, deliberate, and vote.

81. A judicatory is not necessarily bound to give a final judgment in a case of Reference, but may remit the whole case, either with or without advice, to the inferior judicatory.

82. The whole record of proceedings shall be promptly transmitted to the superior judicatory, and, if the Reference is accepted, the parties shall be heard.

### III. OF COMPLAINTS.

83. A Complaint is a written representation, made to the next superior judicatory, by one or more persons subject and submitting to the jurisdiction of the judicatory complained of, respecting any delinquency, or any decision, by an inferior judicatory.

84. Written notice of Complaint, with the reasons therefor, shall be given, within ten days after the action was taken, to the Clerk, or, in case of his death, absence, or disability, to the Moderator, of the judicatory complained of, who shall lodge it, with the records and all the papers pertaining to the case, with the Clerk of the superior judicatory, be-

fore the close of the second day of its regular meeting next ensuing the date of the reception of said notice.

85. Whenever a Complaint, in cases non-judicial, is entered against a decision of a judicatory, signed by at least one-third of the members recorded as present when the action was taken, the execution of such decision shall be stayed, until the final issue of the case by the superior judicatory.

86. The complainant shall lodge his Complaint, and the reasons therefor, with the Clerk of the superior judicatory before the close of the second day of its meeting next ensuing the date of the notice thereof.

87. If the higher judicatory finds that the Complaint is in order, and that sufficient reasons for proceeding to trial have been assigned, the next step shall be to read the record of the action complained of, and so much of the record of the lower judicatory as may be pertinent; then the parties shall be heard, and, after that, the judicatory shall proceed to consider and determine the case, as provided for in cases of original process. In cases of Complaint involving a judicial decision, proceedings in an appellate judicatory shall be had in the order and as provided in Section 100, Chapter IV., entitled "Of Appeals."

88. The effect of a Complaint, if sustained, may be the reversal, in whole or in part, of the action of the lower judicatory; and may

also, in cases non-judicial, be the infliction of censure upon the judicatory complained of. When a Complaint is sustained, the lower judicatory shall be directed how to dispose of the matter.

89. The parties to a Complaint, in cases non-judicial, shall be known, respectively, as Complainant and Respondent—the latter being the judicatory complained of, which should always be represented by one or more of its number appointed for that purpose, who may be assisted by counsel.

90. Neither the Complainant nor the members of the judicatory complained of shall sit, deliberate, or vote in the case.

91. Either of the parties to a Complaint may appeal to the next superior judicatory, except as limited by Chapter XI., Section 4, of the Form of Government.

92. The judicatory against which a Complaint is made shall send up its records, and all the papers relating to the matter of the Complaint, and filed with the record; and, for failure to do this, it shall be censured by the superior judicatory, which shall have power to make such orders, pending the production of the records and papers, and the determination of the Complaint, as may be necessary to preserve the rights of all the parties.

93. If a case should be carried to an appellate judicatory by both Appeal and Complaint, the same shall be consolidated for trial,

if deemed proper by the appellate judicatory.
If the Appeal be abandoned, the case shall be
heard only on the Complaint.

IV. OF APPEALS.

94. An Appeal is the removal of a judicial
case, by a written representation, from an inferior to a superior judicatory; and may be
taken, by either of the original parties, from
the final judgment of the lower judicatory.
These parties shall be called Appellant and
Appellee.

95. The grounds of Appeal may be such
as these: Irregularity in the proceedings of
the inferior judicatory; refusal to entertain
an Appeal or Complaint; refusal of reasonable indulgence to a party on trial; receiving
improper, or declining to receive important,
testimony; hastening to a decision before the
testimony is fully taken; manifestation of
prejudice in the conduct of the case; and mis-
take or injustice in the decision.

96. Written notice of Appeal, with specifications of the errors alleged, shall be given,
within ten days after the judgment has been
rendered, to the Clerk, or, in case of his death,
absence, or disability, to the Moderator, of the
judicatory appealed from, who shall lodge it,
with the records and all the papers pertaining
to the case, with the Clerk of the superior
judicatory, before the close of the second day

of its regular meeting next ensuing the date
of his reception of said notice.

97. The appellant shall appear in person
or by counsel before the judicatory appealed
to, on or before the close of the second day
of its regular meeting next ensuing the date
of the filing of his notice of Appeal, and shall
lodge his Appeal and specifications of the
errors alleged, with the Clerk of the superior
judicatory, within the time above specified.
If he fail to show to the satisfaction of the
judicatory that he was unavoidably prevented
from so doing, he shall be considered as having abandoned his Appeal, and the judgment
shall stand.

98. Neither the appellant, nor the members
of the judicatory appealed from, shall sit, deliberate, or vote in the case.

99. When due notice of an Appeal has been
given, and the Appeal and the specifications
of the errors alleged have been filed in due
time, the Appeal shall be considered in order.
The judgment, the notice of Appeal, the Appeal, and the specifications of the errors alleged, shall be read; and the judicatory may
then determine, after hearing the parties,
whether the Appeal shall be entertained. If
it be entertained, the following order shall be
observed :

(1) The record in the case, from the begin-
ning, shall be read, except what may be omitted by consent.

(2) The parties shall be heard, the appellant opening and closing.

(3) Opportunity shall be given to the members of the judicatory appealed from to be heard.

(4) Opportunity shall be given to the members of the superior judicatory to be heard.

(5) The vote shall then be separately taken, without debate, on each specification of error alleged, the question being taken in the form : "Shall the specification of error be sustained?" If no one of the specifications be sustained, and no error be found by the judicatory in the record, the judgment of the inferior judicatory shall be affirmed. If one or more errors be found, the judicatory shall determine, whether the judgment of the inferior judicatory shall be reversed or modified, or the case remanded for a new trial ; and the judgment, accompanied by a recital of the error or errors found, shall be entered on the record. If the judicatory deem it wise, an explanatory minute may be adopted which shall be a part of the record of the case.

100. When the judgment directs admonition or rebuke, notice of Appeal shall suspend all further proceedings ; but in other cases the judgments shall be in force until the Appeal is decided.

101. The judicatory whose judgment is appealed from shall send up its records, and all the papers relating thereto, and filed with

the record. If it fails to do this, it shall be censured; and the sentence appealed from shall be suspended, until a record is produced on which the issue can be fairly tried.

102. Appeals are, generally, to be taken to the judicatory immediately superior to that appealed from.

## CHAPTER X.

### OF DISSENTS AND PROTESTS.

103. A DISSENT is a declaration of one or more members of a minority in a judicatory, expressing disagreement with a decision of the majority in a particular case.

104. A Protest is a more formal declaration, made by one or more members of a minority, bearing testimony against what is deemed a mischievous or erroneous proceeding, decision or judgment, and including a statement of the reasons therefor.

105. If a Dissent or Protest be couched in decorous and respectful language, and be without offensive reflections or insinuations against the majority, it shall be entered on the records.

106. The judicatory may prepare an answer to any protest which imputes to it principles or reasonings which its action does not import, and the answer shall also be entered upon the records. Leave may thereupon be

given to the protestant or protestants, if they desire it, to modify their Protest; and the answer of the judicatory may also, in consequence, be modified. This shall end the matter.

107. No one shall be allowed to dissent or protest who has not a right to vote on the question decided,—and, in judicial cases, no one shall be allowed to dissent or protest who did not vote against the decision.

## CHAPTER XI.

### OF JURISDICTION IN CASES OF DISMISSION.

108. THE judicatory, to which a church member or a Minister belongs, shall have sole jurisdiction for the trial of offences whenever or wherever committed by him.

109. A member of a Church, receiving a certificate of dismission to another Church, shall continue to be a member of the Church giving him the certificate, and subject to the jurisdiction of its Session (but shall not deliberate or vote in a church meeting, nor exercise the functions of any office), until he has become a member of the Church to which he is recommended, or some other evangelical Church; and, should he return the certificate, within a year from its date, the Session shall make record of the fact, but he shall not thereby be restored to the exercise of the

functions of any office previously held by him in that Church.

110. In like manner, a Minister shall be subject to the jurisdiction of the Presbytery which dismissed him (but shall not deliberate or vote, nor be counted in the basis of representation to the General Assembly), until he actually becomes a member of another Presbytery; but, should he return the certificate of dismission within a year from its date, the Presbytery shall make record of the fact, and restore him to the full privileges of membership.

111. A Presbytery, giving a certificate of dismission to a Minister, Licentiate, or Candidate for licensure, shall specify the particular body to which he is recommended; and, if recommended to a Presbytery, no other than the one designated, if existing, shall receive him.

112. If a Church becomes extinct, the Presbytery with which it was connected shall have jurisdiction over its members, and grant them letters of dismission to some other Church. It shall, also, determine any case of discipline begun by the Session and not concluded.

113. If a Presbytery becomes extinct, the Synod, with which it was connected, shall have jurisdiction over its members, and may transfer them to any Presbytery within its bounds. It shall, also, determine any case of discipline begun by the Presbytery and not concluded.

# CHAPTER XII.

## OF REMOVALS, AND LIMITATION OF TIME.

**114.** WHEN any member shall remove from one Church to another, he shall produce a certificate, ordinarily not more than one year old, of his church-membership and dismission, before he shall be admitted as a regular member of that Church.

The names of the baptized children of a parent seeking dismission to another Church shall, if such children are members of his household and remove with him and are not themselves communicants, be included in the certificate of dismission. The certificate shall be addressed to a particular Church, and the fact of the reception of the person or persons named in it shall be promptly communicated to the Church which gave it.

**115.** In like manner, when a Minister, Licentiate, or Candidate, is dismissed from one Presbytery to another, the certificate shall be presented to the Presbytery, to which it is addressed, ordinarily within one year from its date, and the fact of his reception shall be promptly communicated to the Presbytery dismissing him.

**116.** If a church-member, more than two years absent from the place of his ordinary residence and Church connections, applies for a certificate of membership, his absence, and the knowledge of the Church respecting his demeanor for that time, or its want of information concerning it, shall be distinctly stated in the certificate.

117. Prosecution for an alleged offence shall commence within one year from the time of its alleged commission, or from the date when it becomes known to the judicatory which has jurisdiction thereof.

---

# CHAPTER XIII.

## JUDICIAL COMMISSIONS.

118. THE General Assembly, and each Synod under its care, shall have power to appoint a Judicial Commission from their respective bodies, consisting of ministers and elders, in number not less than a quorum of the judicatory appointing.

All judicial cases may be submitted to this Commission, and its decisions shall be final, except in matters of law, which shall be referred to the appointing court for final adjudication; and also all matters of Constitution and Doctrine, which may be reviewed in the appointing body, and upon final adjudication by the General Assembly. The Commission shall sit at the same time and place as the body appointing it, and its findings shall be entered upon the minutes of such body.

# DIRECTORY FOR WORSHIP.

## CHAPTER X.

### OF THE MODE OF INFLICTING AND REMOVING CEN-SURES.

I. THE power which Christ has given the rulers of his Church is for edification, and not destruction. When, therefore, a communicant shall have been found guilty of a fault deserving censure, the judicatory shall proceed with all tenderness, and restore the offending brother in the spirit of meekness, its members considering themselves, lest they also be tempted. Censure ought to be inflicted with great solemnity; that it may be the means of impressing the mind of the delinquent with a proper sense of his sin; and that, with the divine blessing, it may lead him to repentance.

II. When the judicatory has resolved to pass sentence, suspending a communicant from church privileges, the Moderator shall pronounce the sentence in the following form:

"Whereas you have been found guilty [*by your own confession, or by sufficient proof, as the case may be*] of the sin of [*here mention the particular offence*], we declare you suspended from the sacrament of the Lord's Supper, till you give satisfactory evidence of repentance."

To this shall be added such advice, admonition, or rebuke, as may be judged neces-

512

sary; and the whole shall be concluded with prayer to Almighty God, that he would follow this act of discipline with his blessing. In general, such censure should be inflicted in the presence of the judicatory only; but, if the judicatory think it expedient to rebuke the offender publicly, this solemn suspension may be in the presence of the Church.

III. After a person has been thus suspended, the Minister and Elders should frequently converse with him, as well as pray for him in private, that it would please God to give him repentance. And, particularly on days preparatory to the dispensing of the Lord's Supper, the prayers of the Church should be offered up for those who have shut themselves out from this holy communion.

IV. When the judicatory shall be satisfied as to the reality of the repentance of any suspended member, he shall be allowed to profess his repentance, and be restored to fellowship, in the presence of the Session, or of the Church.

V. When a suspended person has failed to manifest repentance for his offence, and has continued in obstinate impenitence not less than a year, it may become the duty of the judicatory to excommunicate him without further trial. The design of excommunication is to operate upon the offender as a means of reclaiming him, to deliver the Church from the scandal of his offence, and to inspire all with fear by the example of his punishment.

VI. When a judgment of excommunication is to be executed, with or without previous suspension, it is proper that the sentence be publicly pronounced against the offender.

The Minister shall, therefore, at a regular meeting of the Church, make a brief statement of the several steps which have been taken, with respect to the offender, announcing that it has been found necessary to excommunicate him.

He shall begin by showing (from Matt. xviii. 15, 16, 17, 18; 1 Cor. v. 1, 2, 3, 4, 5) the power of the Church to cast out unworthy members, and shall briefly explain the nature, use, and consequences of this censure.

Then he shall pronounce the sentence in the following or like form, viz. :

"Whereas A. B. hath been, by sufficient proof, convicted of [*here insert the sin*], and after much admonition and prayer refuseth to hear the Church, and hath manifested no evidence of repentance ; therefore, in the name, and by the authority, of the Lord Jesus Christ, I pronounce him to be excluded from the communion of this Church."

After which, prayer shall be made for the conviction and reformation of the excommunicated person, and for the establishment of all true believers.

But the judicatory may omit the publication of the excommunication, when it judges that there is sufficient reason for such omission.

VII. When an excommunicated person shall be so affected by his state as to be brought to repentance, and desires to be re-admitted to the privileges of the Church, the Session of the Church which excommunicated him, having obtained, and placed on record, sufficient evidence of his sincere repentance and deep contrition, shall proceed to restore him, recording, in explicit terms, the grounds on which such conclusion has been reached.

The sentence of restoration shall be pronounced by the Minister, at a regular meeting of the Church on the Lord's Day, in the following words:

"Whereas A. B. has been excluded from the communion of the Church, but has now given satisfactory evidence of repentance; in the name of the Lord Jesus Christ, and by his authority, I declare him absolved from the sentence of excommunication formerly pronounced against him; and I do restore him to the communion of the Church, that he may be a partaker of all the benefits of the Lord Jesus, to his eternal salvation."

After which, he shall be commended to God in prayer.

VIII. Censures, other than suspension from church privileges, or excommunication, shall be inflicted in such mode as the judicatory may direct.

# INDEX.

[Figures, thus (28), refer to sections of Book of Discipline, and thus (II.), to sections of Chap. X. Dir. of Worship.]

(516)

44

44 *

THE END.

## EXTRACT FROM THE MINUTES OF THE GENERAL ASSEMBLY FOR 1885.

*Resolved,* That the Board of Publication be directed, under the direction of the Stated Clerk, to publish a pamphlet edition of the REVISED BOOK OF DISCIPLINE, and that the said Board be also directed to send gratuitously by mail two copies of said pamphlet to every pastor and stated supply upon the roll of ministers, and one copy to every unemployed minister and vacant church, and said pastors and stated supplies be enjoined, upon the reception of the two copies indicated, to lay one of them before the session.

Attest,　　WM. II. ROBERTS,

*Stated Clerk.*

PRINCETON, N. J., June 18, 1885.


## MINUTE ADOPTED BY THE GENERAL ASSEMBLY OF 1884 WITH REFERENCE TO THE COMMITTEE ON THE REVISION OF THE BOOK OF DISCIPLINE.

The Rev. Elijah R. Craven, D. D., Chairman of the Committee on the Revision of the Book of Discipline, asked that the Committee, having performed the task assigned it, be now discharged. The request was granted, with the unanimous thanks of the Assembly.


## EXTRACT FROM THE MINUTES OF THE GENERAL ASSEMBLY OF 1880.

The Committee (on Revision) consists of the following named persons:

*Ministers.*—Elijah R. Craven, Edwin F. Hatfield, Alexander T. McGill, William E. Moore, Nathaniel West, Robert W. Patterson, Francis L. Patton.

*Elders.*—William Strong, Joseph Allison, Samuel M. Breckenridge, Samuel M. Moore, John T. Nixon.

www.ingramcontent.com/pod-product-compliance
Lightning Source LLC
Chambersburg PA
CBHW021428090426
42739CB00009B/1393